Future Tech

The Future of

Cities

Kevin Kurtz

Lerner Publications ◆ Minneapolis

To my city-dwelling stepsister Jill

Lerner Publications Company
An imprint of Lerner Publishing Group, Inc.
241 First Avenue North
Minneapolis, MN 55401 USA

For reading levels and more information, look up this title at www.lernerbooks.com.

Main body text set in Adrianna Regular.
Typeface provided by Chank.

Editor: Rebecca Higgins **Designer**: Amy Salveson **Photo Editor**: Rebecca Higgins

Library of Congress Cataloging-in-Publication Data

Names: Kurtz, Kevin, author.
Title: The future of cities / Kevin Kurtz.
Description: Minneapolis : Lerner Publications, [2021] | Series: Searchlight books—future tech | Includes bibliographical references and index. | Audience: Ages 8–11 | Audience: Grades K–1 | Summary: "With Earth's population growing and water levels rising, city engineers will have to fit more people on less land. Discover rooftop farms, floating cities, and more" — Provided by publisher.
Identifiers: LCCN 2019046345 (print) | LCCN 2019046346 (ebook) | ISBN 9781541597334 (library binding) | ISBN 9781728413785 (paperback) | ISBN 9781728400792 (ebook)
Subjects: LCSH: Cities and towns—Juvenile literature. | Smart cities—Juvenile literature.
Classification: LCC HT152 .K87 2020 (print) | LCC HT152 (ebook) | DDC 307.76—dc23

LC record available at https://lccn.loc.gov/2019046345
LC ebook record available at https://lccn.loc.gov/2019046346

Manufactured in the United States of America
1-47837-48277-1/31/2020

Contents

Chapter 1

THE FUTURE IS URBAN

Imagine waking up after a blizzard and seeing no snow outside. The streets automatically heated up and melted the snow away. When you go to a café, a robot pours your coffee. You pay for it by walking out the door. When you throw the cup away, it gets sucked through an underground tube. It travels to a landfill blocks away. Then you call a drone. It picks you up and takes you where you need to go. These are just some of the ways a city may work in the future.

These robots prepare and serve coffee.

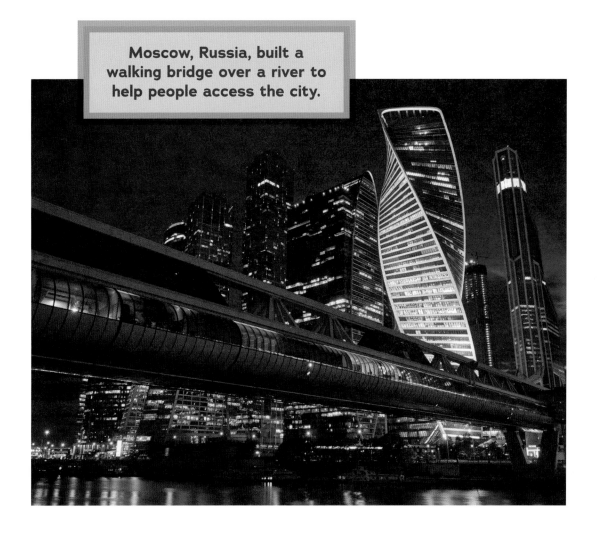

Moscow, Russia, built a walking bridge over a river to help people access the city.

Changing World, Changing Cities

Cities are changing to take advantage of new technologies. A city isn't just a place where lots of people live. It needs to provide homes, food, water, energy, transportation, waste removal, and other services to everyone that lives there. New technologies could make it easier for cities to provide these services.

Three million people pass through Istiklal Street every day in Istanbul, Turkey.

Cities need to meet future challenges too. The world's population is rising quickly. In 2050, seven billion people will live in cities, compared to four billion people in 2019. Cities will have to provide for the needs of their growing populations.

Meanwhile, problems related to global climate change will continue. Cities need to figure out how to reduce their impact on the environment. They will also need to adjust to changes such as rising sea levels.

MELTING GLACIERS ARE ADDING TO RISING SEA LEVELS.

Smart meters show where electricity is being used.

The Future Is Now

The most populated city in the world is Tokyo, Japan. It provides thirty-seven million people with everything they need to live. Tokyo is installing electricity meters around the city. The meters will pinpoint places in the city where energy is being wasted. Finding these places will help the city reduce energy consumption and pollution. Modern city solutions can provide a window into what cities of the future will be like.

Chapter 2

A HOME IN THE CITY

Cities fit many people into small spaces. The most populated parts of New York City have about 143 people for every football field-sized area of land. Cities provide enough homes through multistory buildings. The biggest residential building in the world is the Edifício Copan in São Paulo, Brazil. It is thirty-eight stories high, has 1,160 apartments, and is home to five thousand people!

The Edifício Copan is home to so many residents that it has its own zip code.

The Future of Skyscrapers

Future cities will need more high-rise buildings to accommodate everyone. Unfortunately, skyscrapers are a major source of greenhouse gases. Greenhouse gases stay in the atmosphere and trap heat from the sun. Construction materials create about 10 percent of our total emissions. Heating, cooling, and powering skyscrapers also creates a lot of greenhouse gases.

Some skyscrapers are trying to reduce their emissions.

The Walbrook Building in London, England, uses solar shading to keep it cool in the summer and warm in the winter.

Future skyscrapers will produce little to no greenhouse gases. Many will have wind turbines on their roofs. The turbines will make clean energy to power the buildings. Thin, see-through solar panels could be placed on the building's windows. They would collect the sun's energy and turn it into electricity.

New skyscrapers will be made with environmentally friendly materials. Engineers have developed a way to glue wood together to create an amazing new type of timber. The timber is as strong as steel! It is better for the environment than steel and concrete.

Concrete is responsible for 4 to 8 percent of the world's carbon dioxide emissions.

No fossil fuels were burned when this timber was made.

The greenhouse gas carbon dioxide is the biggest driver of climate change. Trees and other plants pull carbon dioxide out of the air. The carbon becomes part of the tree's wood. When skyscrapers are made of wood, the wood's carbon can't go back into the atmosphere. Of course, cutting down trees is not good for the environment. But new trees can be planted to replace the trees used in the buildings.

Cities Rise with the Sea

Many cities are by the ocean. Climate change is causing the sea level to rise. Coastal cities such as Miami and Singapore will likely be flooded by the end of this century. These cities need to figure out ways to remain livable. Otherwise, all their people will have to move.

Rising sea levels could flood hundreds of cities.

Flooding in coastal cities will be worse during daily high tides. It may go away during low tides. Some cities may need buildings that can float during high tide. The buildings could be attached to poles so they don't float away. They would gently float up and then float back down as the tide goes out.

St. Mark's Square in Venice, Italy, floods during high tide.

Floating cities will have to figure out what to do with their trash to prevent it from floating in the ocean.

Some coastal cities may eventually become floating cities. Buildings could be constructed on platforms that float permanently on the ocean. As the sea level keeps rising, new platforms could be added to older ones. This could keep cities above rising waters.

Chapter 3

THE ESSENTIALS OF LIFE

Cities need to make sure millions of people get food and water every day. Food almost always comes from farms. Some of these farms may be on other continents.

Unfortunately, the fuel used to ship food creates a lot of greenhouse gases. Climate change causes floods and droughts that damage farmlands. This could make it harder for cities to get enough food.

Some farms are already feeling the effects of climate change such as more severe storms.

Vertical farms can save time and energy used to transport foods.

To meet these challenges, many future cities will grow their own food. Gardens and crops will grow on the roofs of buildings. Some will grow indoors in vertical farms. Vertical farms don't need sunlight. The plants grow on shelves under ultraviolet light bulbs. The light bulbs could be powered by pollution-free wind and solar energy. Skyscrapers might have entire floors for vertical farms. These farms can also be built underneath the city. In the future, your vegetables may be grown in your apartment building.

A Drop to Drink?

Many places on Earth are running out of water. Over 96 percent of Earth's water is undrinkable salt water. Some cities get enough rain to refill their freshwater supplies. Cities in dry areas such as Los Angeles, California, get water from glaciers in nearby mountains. Other cities get water from underground.

Water purification plants ensure that water is drinkable and free of harmful elements.

Climate change is melting glaciers and causing droughts. These changes and decades of overuse are causing cities' water supplies to disappear. As glaciers melt away and groundwater dries up, cities will need to look elsewhere for water.

CITIES ALSO HAVE TO FIGHT WATER POLLUTION.

▼

A desalination plant in California costs $1 billion to build.

As drinkable water becomes harder to get, more and more coastal cities will need desalination plants. Desalination plants turn ocean water into fresh water. Unfortunately, desalination plants are too expensive to run for most cities.

At desalination plants, machines turn salt water into fresh water.

Desalination plants also have serious environmental problems. They require a lot of energy. This can add more greenhouse gases to the atmosphere. They suck in millions of gallons of ocean water and sometimes harm aquatic animals. The plants pump dirty wastewater back into the oceans, which can seriously impact marine wildlife. Scientists are searching for solutions to these issues.

future of Ew!

The water we drink and clean with does not just disappear. It goes down drains to wastewater treatment plants. The plants clean the water and put it back into the environment. Since many cities are running out of water, treatment plants may need new technologies to turn wastewater into drinkable water. In the future, the water flushed down your neighbors' toilets could eventually come back to your house for you to drink.

Some cities are already reusing water. They get their water from a river that another city dumps wastewater into.

Chapter 4

SMART CITIES

Many of us have smartphones, smart appliances, and smart homes. In the future, we may have smart cities too. A smart city will have computers to run its basic services. For example, streetlights will automatically report when a bulb is out. The bulb can then be quickly replaced. Streets could detect when snow and ice are covering them and melt it away. Street sensors could tell your car where the nearest parking spot is. That way, you don't have to drive around looking for one.

The average US driver spends seventeen hours a year looking for a parking spot.

STEM Spotlight

In the future, city garbage may not be collected by people. Instead, it may be sucked away by underground pneumatic tubes. Pneumatic tubes work by creating a vacuum at one end. A vacuum is a space with nothing in it—not even air. This creates a pressure difference between the tubes and the vacuum. The difference allows the garbage to blast through the tubes at over 60 miles (97 km) per hour. A couple of minutes later, the garbage shoots out into a landfill.

Pneumatic tubes can transport things quickly.

Computers in Charge

Computers will not only run citywide services. They will also run stores and other businesses. Sensors will scan the items you buy as you walk out of a store. They then charge the payment to your phone. Computers may even drive all the cars in the city. You could use an app to call a car to pick you up. Driverless drones may fill the skies. These drones will be like flying taxis taking you where you need to go.

SELF-FLYING DRONES COULD BE FASTER THAN CARS.

Cities could use data to make improvements.

Smart cities will have sensors everywhere. These sensors will constantly monitor people, traffic, and other aspects of city life. They will gather data that computers will analyze. They could then decide things such as when to turn streetlights on or off or which streets have too much traffic. This information will help the city make the best use of space and resources.

Are They That Smart?

Not everyone is a fan of smart cities. Some argue that technology becomes outdated too quickly. It will be too expensive and wasteful to continually replace all these smart-city systems. All the added technology means more things can go wrong. If lighting or traffic computers fail, it can seriously disrupt people's lives. Smart cities need to have sensors and cameras everywhere to collect data. The devices will also be recording what everyone is doing. This will mean people have less privacy.

Predicting the future

The future is never certain. Some of these changes may not happen. But many cities around the world are already taking steps in these directions. Thousands of desalinization plants are operating. Toronto, Canada, is building one of the first smart-city neighborhoods. Roosevelt Island in New York City uses pneumatic garbage collection. The future is already here. As the world keeps changing, the future of cities will need to change too.

Toronto is leading the way into the future of cities.

Glossary

atmosphere: the layer of air that surrounds Earth

carbon dioxide: greenhouse gas released by burning fossil fuels

climate change: normal temperatures and weather patterns changing over time

desalinization: removing salt from salt water to make fresh water

drone: a vehicle that doesn't need a pilot

greenhouse gas: a type of gas in the atmosphere that can trap heat from the sun

pneumatic tube: a human-made tube that transports objects by creating movement through differences in air pressure

pollution: unhealthy chemicals and other substances released into the air and water by human activity

sensor: a device that observes and measures conditions such as temperature, movement, and light

ultraviolet light: a type of radiation released by the sun and certain light bulbs that plants need

wastewater: water made dirty by human activity

Learn More about the Future of Cities

Books

Chambers, Catherine. *Stickmen's Guide to Cities in Layers*. Minneapolis: Hungry Tomato, 2017. Discover cities from the highest skyscrapers to underground sewers.

Kurtz, Kevin. *Climate Change and Rising Seas*. Minneapolis: Lerner Publications, 2019. Find out more about climate change and why some coastal cities may be in danger of flooding.

Lonely Planet staff. *The Cities Book*. Oakland: Lonely Planet, 2016. Travel to two hundred exciting cities around the world.

Websites

Engineering: Go for It
http://www.egfi-k12.org
Explore engineering and how to build a greener world.

Kiddle: Urbanization Facts
https://kids.kiddle.co/Urbanization
Learn more about the rising population in cities.

Plan It Green: The Big Switch
https://games4sustainability.org/gamepedia/plan-it-green-the-big
-switch/
Build your own city and tackle challenges while keeping your citizens happy.

Index

Photo Acknowledgments

Image credits: SRAVIN THUNHIKORN/Shutterstock.com, p. 4; Max Ryazanov/Getty Images, p. 5; Ayhan Altun/Getty Images, p. 6; Andrea Toffaletti/500px/Getty Images, p. 7; Ulrich Baumgarten/Getty Images, p. 8; Rick Gerharter/Getty Images, p. 9; Xuanyu Han/Getty Images, p. 10; View Pictures/Getty Images, p. 11; Thn K Vt Phu Ceriy/EyeEm/Getty Images, p. 12; View Pictures/Getty Images, p. 13; John Seaton Callahan/Getty Images, p. 14; Matteo Colombo/Getty Images, p. 15; Eloi_Omella/Getty Images, p. 16; Steve Denton/EyeEm/Getty Images, p. 17; LouisHiemstra/Getty Images, p. 18; Bim/Getty Images, p. 19; wasja/Getty Images, p. 20; tanukiphoto/Getty Images, p. 21; Andy Sotiriou/Getty Images, p. 22; Andersen Ross Photography Inc/Getty Images, p. 23; Gail Shotlander/Getty Images, p. 24; primeimages/Getty Images, p. 25; Chesky/Shutterstock.com, p. 26; dowell/Getty Images, p. 27; Fotoholica Press/Getty Images, p. 28; Safwat Ghabbour/Getty Images, p. 29.

Cover: GlobalVision Communication/GlobalVision 360/Getty Images.